# Animal Peculiarity Volume 3 Part 6

*By T.P Just*

~~~

## Copyright © 2010 by Terence Just. All rights reserved.

## Get All The Books In The Series:

Animal Peculiarity Volume 1 Part [1-8]
Animal Peculiarity Volume 2 Part [1-8]
Animal Peculiarity Volume 3 Part [1-8]
**<u>Just Enterprises</u>**

I0436331

# Table of Contents

# 1. Introduction

The unique characteristics of animals is a miscellany of facts, genuine or supposed, gleamed from earlier and contemporary Greek writers (No Latin writer is once named) and to a limited extent from his own observation to illustrate the habits of the animal world.

We are of course prepared to encounter much that modern science rejects, but the general tone with its search after the picturesque, the startling, even the miraculous, would justify us in ranking Aelian with the paradoxical, rather than with the sober exponents of natural history.

Mythology, mariners' yarns, vulgar superstitions, the ascertained facts of nature—all serve to adorn a tale and, on occasion, to point a moral. His religion is the popular stoicism of the age. Aleian repeatedly affirms his belief in the gods and in divine providence; the wisdom and beneficence of Nature are held up to veneration; the folly and selfishness of man are contrasted with the untaught virtues of the animal world. Some animals, to be sure, have their failings, but he chooses rather to dwell upon their good qualities, devotion, courage, self-sacrifice, gratitude. Again, animals are guided by reason, and from them we may learn contentment, control of the passions, and calm in the face of death.

His primary object is to entertain and while so doing to convey instruction in the most agreeable form. Some might find fault with his random and piece-meal handling of his theme-of which he is well aware, and he defends himself with the plea that a frequent change of topic helps to maintain the reader's interest and saves him from boredom.

As to the permanent value of his work he has no misgivings and since we have been informed that his writings were much admired, we may assume that they appealed to cultivated circles in a way that the voluminous and possibly arid compilations of grammarians did not.

Now I am well aware of the labour that others have expended on this subject, yet I have collected all the materials that I could; I have clothed them in untechnical language, and am persuaded that my achievement is a treasure far from negligible. So if anyone considers them profitable, let him make use of them; anyone who does not consider them so may give them to his father to keep and attend to.

# 2. The Elephant as bodyguard

When the Indian King sets forth to administer justice an Elephant first bows down before him: it has been taught to do so and remembers perfectly and, obeys.
(At it stands the man who teaches it to remember its instruction by a stroke from his goad and by some words in his native speech which thanks to a mysterious gift of nature peculiar to this animal the Elephant can understand.)
Moreover it executes some warlike motion, as though it would show that it recollects this part of its teaching also Four and twenty Elephants take it in turn to stand sentry over the King, just like the other guards, and are taught to keep watch and not to fall asleep : for this lesson also they are taught by Indian skill.

And Hecataeus of Miletus says that Amphiaraus, the son of Oicles, went to sleep during his watch and suffered the fate which he describes. These animals however are wakeful and are not overcome by sleep; they are the most trustworthy of the guards there, at any rate next to human beings.

# 3. The Sea Scolopendra

Now in the course of examining and investigating these subjects and what bears upon them, to the Utmost limit, with all the zeal that I could command, I have ascertained that the Scolopendra is sea-monster, and of sea-monsters it is the biggest, and if cast up on the shore no one would have the courage to look at it.

And those who are expert in marine matters say that they have seen them floating and that they extend the whole of their head above the sea, exposing hairs of immense length protruding from their nostrils, and that the tail is flat and resembles that of a crayfish.

And at times the rest of their body is to be seen floating on the surface, and its bulk is comparable to a full-sized trireme. And they swim with numerous feet in line on either side as though they were rowing themselves (though the expression is somewhat harsh) with tholepins hung alongside.

So those who have experience in these matters say that the surge responds with a gentle murmur, and their statement convinces me.

# 4. Xenophon on Hounds

Xenophon has also the following remarks touching Hounds
You should take them to the mountains frequently, but less
frequently on to fields. For the beaten tracks on cultivated
lands injure and mislead them.

And the same writer says that it is better to take them on to
rough ground, and points out the additional advantage of so
doing, viz that by exercising their bodies their legs gain in
strength and ability to jump.

He also says that in winter the Hare's scent is perceptible for a
long time because of the length of the nights, but in summer
this is so no more, for the opposite reason. The meaning of 'the
opposite' is clear from what has been said above.

# 5. Animals presented to the Indian king

The Indians value Horses and Elephants as animals serviceable under arms and in warfare ; and they value them very highly. At any rate they bring to the King trusses of hay which they throw into the mangers, and fodder which they show to be fresh and undamaged.

And if it is so the King thanks them ; if it is not, he punishes the keepers of the Elephants and the grooms most severely. But he does not reject even other and smaller animals but accepts the following also when brought to him as presents. For the Indians do not disparage any animal whether tame or wild. For example, those of his subjects who hold high office bring him presents of cranes, geese, hens, ducks, turtle-doves, francolins also, partridges, spindaluses (this bird resembles the francolin), and even smaller birds than the afore-named, the boccalis, beccaficos, and what are called ortolans.

And they uncover their gifts and display them, to prove how thoroughly plump they are. They bring also a wealth of fattened stags, of antelopes, of gazelles, and one-horned ,asses, which I have mentioned somewhere earlier on, and different kinds of fish also.

# 6. The Sea Cicada

There is also a Cicada that lives in the sea, and the largest one is like a small crayfish, though neither its horns nor its stings are as long as those of the crayfish. The Sea-cicada is of a darker hue than the crayfish, and when caught appears to squeak.

From beneath its eyes there grow small wings, and these also resemble those of the land-cicada. But few people eat it, since they regard it as sacred. And I have heard that the inhabitants of Seriphus even bury any that is dead when caught; if however a live one falls into their nets, they do not keep it but return it to the sea.

And they even mourn for these creatures when dead and assert that they are the darlings of Perseus the son of Zeus.

# 7. The Hyena fish

The Hyena fish has the same name as the land-hyena. Now if you put its right-hand fin under a man asleep, you will give him a considerable shock. For he will see fearful sights, forms and apparitions, dreams too, sinister and unwelcome.
Further, if you cut off the tail, of a live Horse-mackerel and let the fish go again in the sea, and then attach the aforesaid tail to a mare in foal, she will presently drop her foetus and will miscarry.

# 8. Depilatorie

Again, if a youth wants to keep his chin hairless for as long as possible, the blood of a Tunny rubbed on renders him beardless. And the Torpedo and the Jelly-fish have the same effect, for if their flesh is dissolved in vinegar and rubbed on the cheeks, they say that it banishes hair.

What have those contrivers of evil from Tarentum and Etruria to say to this, men who after experimenting with pitch have discovered that artifice whereby they differentiate men and turn them into women?

# 9. The Gilthead

Of all fishes the Gilthead is the most timid. When the season of neap-tides coincides with Arcturus, the sea recedes from the beach and the sand is left bare and vessels frequently stand high and dry for want of water.

Accordingly the inhabitants take branches of poplar-trees, green and in leaf, and after sharpening them like stakes, fix them in the sand and withdraw. Later the returning tide draws in a countless multitude of the aforesaid fishes ; again it ebbs, leaving a great number of Giltheads in shallow water wherever low-lying or hollow spots may be found, and the fish cower beneath the branches and remain still.

For they are terrified by the branches when the oncoming wind stirs and shakes them, and neither quiver nor dart about. It is quite easy, you might say, for anyone who sets upon the mob of timorous fish to capture and strike them.

At any rate it is not only skilled fishermen that can catch them, but any inexperienced person who chances to be at hand, even children and women.

# 10. Tame Mackerel

In the Ionian Sea close to Epidamnus where the Taulantii live, there is an island and it is called Athena's Isle,' and fisher folk live there. There is also a lagoon in the island where shoals of tame Mackerel are fed.

And the fishermen throw in food to them and observe a treaty of peace with them; so the fish are free and immune from pursuit and attain to a great age; there are even ancient Mackerel living there. Yet they do not feed without making any return, nor do they fail in gratitude for their food, but after they have been fed by the fishermen in the morning they too of their own accord go to join the pursuit, as though they were paying for their maintenance.

And advancing beyond the Harbour they set out to meet the strange Mackerel. When they have encountered them as it were in a company or in line of battle, they swim up to them as being of the same family and the same kind, nor do the strangers flee from them, nor do the tame fish attempt to divert them but bear them company.

Presently the tame fish surround the newcomers, and haying encircled them, close their ranks and cut off the fish in their midst, amounting to a great number, and prevent them from escaping; they wait for their keepers and provide the fishermen with a feast in return for the satisfaction of their own appetites.

For the fishermen arrive, catch the strangers, and perpetrate a massacre. But the tame fish return with all haste to the lagoon, dive into their lairs, and wait for their afternoon meal, which the fishermen bring, if they want allies and loyal friends as fellow-hunters. And this happens every day.

### A cure for Jaundice

Experienced, fishermen teach us that if you give a. cure for a man whose liver is out of order and who is afflicted with jaundice, the gall of a Parrot Wrasse, he will be cured.

# 11. Fishing in shallow waters

Fish are caught without weels or hooks or nets in the following manner. There are many bays in the sea which end in shallows, and one can walk in them. When;, therefore, it is calm and the winds are at rest, skilled fishermen bring a number of people to the spot and then direct them to walk about and trample the sand, throwing all their weight on to the soles of their feet.

As a result deep footprints are left, and if they are preserved and the sand does not collapse and obliterate them, and if the water is not agitated by the wind, after a short interval the fishermen enter and in the trodden hollows and footprints capture flat fish asleep, viz flounders, turbot, plaice, torpedo-fish, and the like.

# 12. Medical properties of sea-urchin and hedgehog

I have spoken earlier on about the Seaurchin and I will now mention what more I have heard. It is also good for the stomach: it helps a man who has been suffering from loss of appetite and loathing every kind of food to regain his strength; it is also a diuretic, according to those who know about these things.

And if you rub it on one who is suffering from the itch, it cures a man hitherto afflicted with the aforesaid disease. And if you burn a Sea-urchin, shell and all, it cleanses suppurating wounds. If you burn a Hedgehog and mingle the ashes with pitch and then rub them on those parts where the hair has fallen off, the fugitives (if I may be allowed the joke) will sprout again.

If drunk with wine, it is good for the kidneys; it is also a cure for dropsy when drunk, as in fact I remarked before. Further, the liver of a Hedgehog, if desiccated by the sun, is a cure for those who suffer from the disease known as elephantiasis.

# 13. Hunting for Elephants tusks

Those who are learned in these matters constantly assert that the tusks of the female Elephant are more valuable than those of the male, and this is what they teach us. In Mauretania Elephants are in the habit of dropping their tusks every tenth year, just as stags drop their horns, though with stags it is every year.

Now these Elephants prefer a level, Well-watered country to any other, and they go down upon their knees and rest their tusks upon the ground in their passionate desire to shed their tusks. And they thrust with such force as finally to bury them in the ground.

Next, with their feet they gently scrape and make smooth the spot that guards their treasure. Now the soil is extremely fertile and in a very short while sends up a crop of grass and effaces the evidence of what occurred for those who pass by. But those who track down these secreted objects and who have some knowledge of the Elephants' designs, bring water in goatskins and disperse them, well filled, in different places, and themselves remain where they are.

And one sleeps while another drinks a little, and I dare say that in the intervals of quaffing from his cup he sings to himself and remembers his sweetheart in his song(Nor should I be surprised if a man tries to seduce some well-grown boy who is with him and is his companion in the quest, for the Moors are handsome, stalwart, and of manly aspect, and are devotees of the chase : and many a heart do they inflame too, while still boys, though they are so big).

So then if those tusks have been buried nearby, by some mysterious and amazing spell they draw the aforesaid water out of the skins and leave them empty. Thereupon the men dig up the ground with mattocks and picks, and the spoil which they have tracked down without the aid of dogs is theirs.

If however the skins remain filled in the place where the tusk-hunters laid them, they go off on a fresh quest and again bring the skins and the water, the instruments of the hunt which I have described.

### The Elephant

The Elephant is even said to possess two hearts and to think double: one heart is the source of anger, the other of gentleness. In saying this I am following accounts given by the Moors.

Moreover the same people constantly affirm the following, namely that there are lynxes and that they are even more snub-nosed than the leopard, and that the tips of their ears are hairy.

The Lynx has a wonderful spring and can maintain the most vigorous and overpowering grip on its catch. So it seems that Euripides bears witness to the unloveliness of this beast when he says somewhere.

> 'And he comes bearing upon his shoulders either the burden of a boar, or the misshapen lynx, a ravening brute ill-conceived.

But why he says 'ill-conceived' is rather a question for the grammarians.

# 14. The Ostrich

Concerning the Ostrich one may also mention The Ostrich the following facts. If you kill an Ostrich and wash out its stomach it will be found to contain pebbles which the bird has swallowed and keeps in its gizzard and in time digests. And these pebbles are an aid to the human digestion; its sinews also and its fat are good for the human sinews.

### Method of Capture

Now the capture of this bird is effected by means of horses, for it runs in a circle keeping to the outer edge, but the horsemen intercept it by keeping on the inner side of the circle, and by wheeling in a narrower compass at length overtake it when it is exhausted with running.

And here is another way to catch it. It builds itself a nest low down on the ground after scooping out the sand with its feet. The centre of the nest is hollow, but it builds up the lips all round and walls off the nest so that the lips may keep out the rain and prevent it from streaming into the nest and deluging the young at a tender age.

It lays over eighty eggs, but does not hatch them simultaneously, nor do they all emerge to daylight at the same time, but while some have already been born, others are still acquiring consistency within the shell. Others again are being kept warm.

When therefore the Ostrich is so engaged, a man-—not a witless person but one who has experience of this kind of hunting—who has seen her, fixes some sharp spears round the nest, planting them upright by the ferrule; and the iron shines.

Then he withdraws and lies in wait to see the result. So the Ostrich returns from her feeding- ground full of love for her chicks arid yearning to be with them. And first of all she casts her eyes around, looking this way and that for fear someone should catch sight of her.

And then overcome and stimulated by her longing, she spreads her wings like a sail and rushing at full speed leaps into her nest to die a most pitiful death entangled and impaled upon the spears. Then the hunter is at hand and seizes the young birds with their mother.

# 15. Eels in the Eretaenus

There is an Italian city in the regions towards the west, and its name is Patavium. They say that the city was the work of Antenor the Trojan.

He founded it, having escaped with his life from; his home when he left his native land after the capture of Troy, because the Greeks had compassion on him, since he saved Menelaus who came with Odysseus as ambassador to treat about Helen, when Antimachus advised that they should be put to death. These were Antimachus's words:

He had accepted the gold of Paris, splendid gifts' as Homer says. Well, there is another city not far away which they call Vicetia, and past it there flows a river of the name of Eretaenus: it traverses a considerable area and then falls into the Eridanus, to which it imparts its waters.

Now in the Eretaenus there are Eels of very great size and far fatter than those from any other place, and this is how they are caught. The fisherman sits upon a' rock jutting out in some bay-like spot on the river where the stream widens out, or else upon a tree which a fierce wind has uprooted and thrown down close to the bank — the tree is beginning to rot and is no use for cutting up and burning.

So the eel-fisher seats himself and taking the intestine of a freshly slaughtered lamb which measures some three or four cubits and has been thoroughly fattened, he lowers one end into the water, and keeps it turning in the eddies;' the other end he holds in his hands, and a piece of reed, the length of a sword-handle, has been inserted into it.

The food does not escape the notice of the Eels, for they delight in this intestine. And the first Eel approaches, stimulated by hunger and with open jaws, and fastening its curved, hook-like teeth, which are hard to disentangle, in the bait, continues to leap up in its efforts to drag it down.

But when the fisherman realises from the agitation of the intestine that the Eel is held fast, he puts the reed to which the intestine has been attached to his mouth and blows down it with all his might, inflating the intestine very considerably. And the down flow of breath distends and swells it. And so the air descends into the Eel, fills its head, fills its windpipe, and stops the creature's breathing.

And as the Eel can neither breathe nor detach its teeth which are fixed in the intestine, it is suffocated, and is drawn up, a victim of the intestine, the blown air, and thirdly of the reed. Now this is a daily occurrence, and many are the Eels caught by many a fisherman. This then is what I have to say of the habits peculiar to these fishes.

# 16. The Sea-lion

We also know that the Sea-lion is in some respects like the crayfish, though we see that the shape of its body is slimmer, with an added dash of dark blue colour; but it is sluggish though possessed of enormous claws resembling; those of crabs.

And it is said by the more experienced fishermen to have certain membranes attached to its shell, and beneath them are some portions of tender flesh which are called lobster-lard. And these benefit mankind: they cleanse a muddy complexion, and if added to oil-of-roses and applied as an ointment, they contribute to a person's beauty and adornment. And I have also heard the following: that the Land-lion is terrified of the monstrous appearance of the Sea- lion and cannot endure the smell of it. And how the same Lion dreads a cock I have explained earlier on.

They say also that if the Sea-lion's shell be ground down and the powder cast into water, and the Land-lion drinks it, he becomes immune from troubles of the stomach. This then is what I have to say of the peculiarities of the Sea-lion.

# 17. The Wild Ass of Mauretania

The Asses of Mauretania gallop at a very great speed, at least at the start they are extremely swift: they seem like a rushing wind or, I do declare, the very wings of a bird. But they quickly tire; their feet weary; their breath fails; they forget their speed; they stand chained to the spot and shed copious tears, not, I think, so much from any fear of impending death as on account of the weakness of their feet.

And so the men leap from their horses and throw halters round the Asses' necks, and each one securing an Ass to his horse, leads the one he has caught like a prisoner of war.

I have said earlier on that the horses of Libya are small in appearance but can gallop at very great speeds

# 18. The wild cattle of Libya

It seems that of Libyan Cattle there are multitudes past numbering, arid those that are wild and roam at large are exceedingly swift. And it often happens that hunters in pursuit of one animal go astray and fall in with others, fresh and untired.

Meantime the hunted animal has plunged into a thicket or a glen and vanished, and others appear, exactly like it, and deceive the sight of the hunter. And if he should start to pursue one of these, he and his horse as well will be the first to give up the chase, for though in course of time he will overtake an animal already weary, he will not overtake those just starting to run: his horse will tire before they do.

Every year these Cattle are caught and slaughtered in great numbers, but their offspring take their place, and they are abundant. And they roam the land with their calves, the bulls along with the cows, some in calf, others with a calf lately born.

If a man captures a calf while still young and does not slaughter it forthwith, he reaps a double advantage, because he captures the mother at the same time if he does what may fittingly be described here:

He makes the calf fast with cord and then leaves it and withdraws. But the cow is wasted with yearning for her child and is goaded with ardent longing, and in her desire to release and carry it off attacks the bonds with her horns, hoping to fret them away and burst them.

But whichever horn she inserts into the tangle of cord she is caught and held fast and remains by her calf, having failed on the one hand to release it, and on the other having entangled herself in bonds from which there is no escape.

So then the hunter after removing the liver for his own use and cutting off the udder, which is still swollen, and flaying the hide, leaves the flesh for the birds and beasts to feed upon. But the calf he takes home entire, for it is extremely pleasant to eat, and also affords rennet which will curdle milk.

# 19. The Weever

The Weever resembles other fishes in all other parts of its
body excepting its head, and that is like the python both in the
size of its eyes (those of the python also are large) and in its
jaws, which to some extent are shaped like the python's.
It has scales too and they are rough, and if one handles them
they feel not unlike the skin of the python. Sharp spines
spring from its body, which contains poison and cause harm if
one, touches them.

# 20. The Indian king, his food

The Indian King by way of dessert eats the same things as, no doubt, the Greeks would desire to eat. But according to Indian; accounts he feasts with the greatest relish upon a certain worm that is begotten in the date-palm, when fried; and they say that he derives such pleasure from the eating. .... . And their accounts convince me.

The following also are additions to his meals, the eggs of swans, of ostriches, and of geese. Now I find no fault with the others, but that he should plot against the offspring and destroy the eggs of swans, the servants of Apollo and, as the common report has it, the most tuneful of birds, is a thing, my dear Indians that I cannot approve.

# 21. The Gazelle of Libya

I have a mind now to relate the following facts The Gazelle touching the Gazelles and Prickets of Libya. The Gazelles are very swift-footed; for all that they cannot outrun the Libyan horses. They are also caught with nets. The belly is grey, and this colour extends upwards to their flanks; arid on either side of the belly black stripes creep down their bodies.
The rest of the body however is light- brown; the legs are long; the eyes black; the head is adorned with horns; the ears are very long. But the Pricket, as poets call it, runneth very swiftly, even as the hurricane in appearance it is red and very shaggy, but its tail is white; its eyes are the colour of dark blue dye; its ears are filled with very thick hair; its horns incline forwards and are graceful, so that the creature conies on and while inspiring fear, is a thing of beauty.

Now this Pricket does not display its speed only on land, but will plunge into a running river and cleave the stream by rowing, so to speak, with its hooves. And it loves to swim in a lake, and there, let me tell you, it obtains food, and feasts upon the ever-flowering rush and galingale. So at the beginning of spring it empties its full belly; its udder drops and it suckles its young.

### The 'Myras'

There is, X learn, a fish called *Myrus*, but from what source it has derived its name I cannot say. At any rate that is the name by which it is called. And they say that it is a sea-snake.

### And its eye

Now if and its eye one takes out either of its eyes and wears it as an amulet, it cures a man of dry ophthalmia; but the Myrus, they say, grows a fresh eye. But you must let the fish go alive; otherwise you will preserve its eye to no purpose.

**Get All The Books In The Series:**

Animal Peculiarity Volume 1 Part [1-8]
Animal Peculiarity Volume 2 Part [1-8]
Animal Peculiarity Volume 3 Part [1-8]